KU-152-887

How Toys Work

# Pulleys

| ABERDEENSHIRE LIBRARIES | |
| --- | --- |
| 3156777 | |
| Bertrams | 28/01/2015 |
| J621.85 | £11.99 |
| | |

## Siân Smith

**www.raintreepublishers.co.uk**
Visit our website to find out more information about Raintree books.

**To order:**
☎ Phone 0845 6044371
📄 Fax +44 (0) 1865 312263
✉ Email myorders@raintreepublishers.co.uk

Customers from outside the UK please telephone +44 1865 312262

Raintree is an imprint of Capstone Global Library Limited, a company incorporated in England and Wales having its registered office at 7 Pilgrim Street, London, EC4V 6LB – Registered company number: 6695582

Text © Capstone Global Library Limited 2013
First published in hardback in 2013
The moral rights of the proprietor have been asserted.

All rights reserved. No part of this publication may be reproduced in any form or by any means (including photocopying or storing it in any medium by electronic means and whether or not transiently or incidentally to some other use of this publication) without the written permission of the copyright owner, except in accordance with the provisions of the Copyright, Designs and Patents Act 1988 or under the terms of a licence issued by the Copyright Licensing Agency, Saffron House, 6–10 Kirby Street, London EC1N 8TS (www.cla.co.uk). Applications for the copyright owner's written permission should be addressed to the publisher.

Edited by Dan Nunn, Rebecca Rissman, and Sian Smith
Designed by Joanna Hinton-Malivoire
Picture research by Mica Brancic
Production by Victoria Fitzgerald
Originated by Capstone Global Library Ltd
Printed and bound in China by South China Printing Company Ltd

ISBN 978 1 4062 3799 3
16 15 14 13 12
10 9 8 7 6 5 4 3 2 1

**British Library Cataloguing in Publication Data**
Smith, Sian.
Pulleys. -- (How toys work)
1. Pulleys--Juvenile literature.
I. Title II. Series
621.8'5-dc22

**Acknowledgements**
The author and publisher are grateful to the following for permission to reproduce copyright material: © Capstone Global Library Ltd pp.5, 6, 7, 8, 9, 11, 22b, 23 bottom (Karon Dubke ), 12, 13, 14, 15, 18, 19, 20, 21, 23 top (Lord and Leverett), 16, 17 (Tudor Photography); Shutterstock pp.4 top left (© Galchenkova Ludmila, 4 bottom right (© Gorilla), 4 top right (© Hirurg), 4 bottom left (© Ron Zmiri), 10 (© Alberto Tirado), 22a (© Cheryl Casey), 22c (© bluecrayola), 22d (© Dikiiy).

Cover photograph of a boy on a zip line reproduced with permission of Corbis (© moodboard). Back cover photograph of a toy crane reproduced with permission of © Capstone Publishers (Karon Dubke).

We would like to thank David Harrison, Nancy Harris, Dee Reid, and Diana Bentley for their assistance in the preparation of this book.

Every effort has been made to contact copyright holders of material reproduced in this book. Any omissions will be rectified in subsequent printings if notice is given to the publisher.

# Contents

# Different toys

There are many different kinds of toys.

Toys work in different ways.

# Pulleys

pulley

Some toys use pulleys.

wheel

rope

A pulley is a wheel with a rope around it.

You can pull one end of the rope
to lift something up.

You can let go of the rope to move something down.

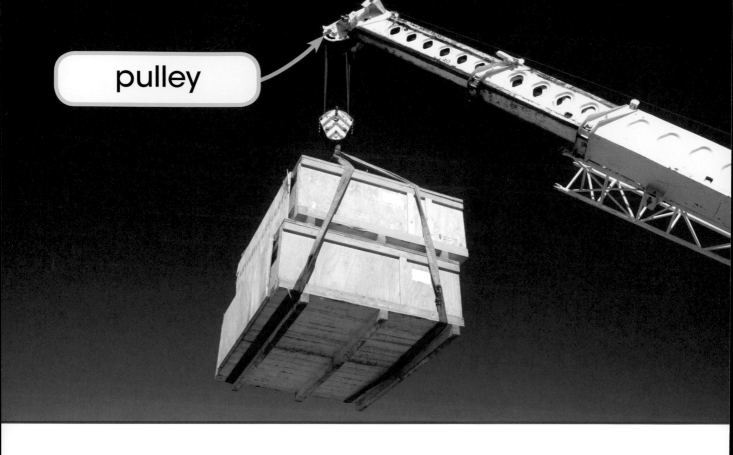

**pulley**

A pulley can help us to lift
heavy things.

A toy crane uses a pulley to
lift things.

small pulley

big pulley

A big pulley and a small pulley can be joined together.

It is harder to push the big pulley.

But it makes the small pulley turn fast.

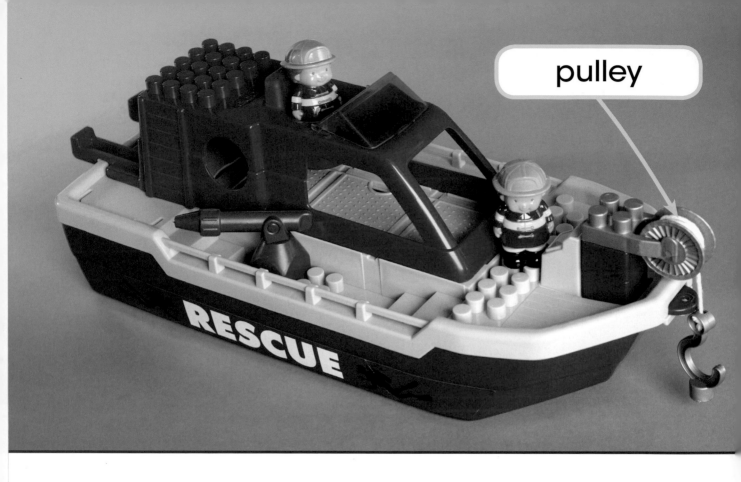

pulley

This toy boat works with a pulley.

lifeboat

The pulley lifts lifeboats up
and down.

pulley

This toy truck works with a pulley.

The pulley lifts cars up and down.

# Quiz

Which one of these toys uses a pulley to work?

22

Answer on page 24

# Picture glossary

**drive belt**  a band that wraps around two wheels. It joins the wheels so that when one wheel turns, the other does too.

**pulley**  a wheel with a rope around it. We use pulleys to help us lift things up or put them down.

# Index

Answer to question on page 22: Toy b uses a pulley to work.

## Notes for parents and teachers
### Introduction
Show the children a collection of toys. One or more of the toys should have a pulley mechanism. Ask the children if they can spot the toy with the pulley. Alternatively show the children pictures of pulleys, for example those used on a flagpole, a boat, and a crane. Do they know what a pulley is and what it does?

### More information about pulleys
Explain that a pulley is a wheel with a rope, chain, or belt wrapped around it. Show the children an example of a grooved pulley wheel and explain that many pulleys have a dip or groove around the edge of the wheel to stop the rope, chain, or belt from slipping off the sides. A pulley is a simple machine that helps us to lift things up or lower them down. Pulleys also make it easier for us to lift or move heavy things.

### Follow up activities
Support the children in using a construction set to create a working pulley. For example, you could make a simple crane and use this to lift something, or make a windmill similar to the one on page 15. For more advanced work on simple machines, children can work with an adult to discuss and play the games at: www.edheads.org/activities/simple-machines

24